Reefer Madness

June 17, 2021

For Glenn

Reefer Madness

Poems by

Robert Cooperman

Have a high old
time,

love,

Bob

Cover design by Shay Culligan

ISBN: 978-1-954353-68-8

Kelsay Books
502 South 1040 East, A-119
American Fork, Utah, 84003

For Beth, As Always

Acknowledgments

The author wishes to thank the editors of the following reviews, where some of these poems, in earlier form, first appeared.

Abbey: "Nancy Tolliver Buys Girl Scout Cookies Outside the Wild Weed"

Blue Collar Review: "Now That It's Legal"

CreativityZine: "The Lid," "Druggie Songs," "Jimi, 1974"

Dope Fiend Daily: "Rolling Joints"

Gargoyle: "Worse," "Melvin Dickson, the Girl Scouts, and Pot Shops"

Glimpse: "Deidre Gleeson, Mother of Vicki," "Brad Whitaker Waits at His Girlfriend's House"

Horror Sleaze Trash: "Thomas Bickerstaff Buys Girl Scout Cookies Outside the Wild Weed"

Illuminations: "Skunk Hour"

Main Street Rag: "Gerald Lockhart Walks Past the Wild Weed"

Poetalk: "Franklin Ambrose, Single Father, Chaperoning His Girl Scout Daughter Elise," "Elise Ambrose, Girl Scout, Denver, Colorado"

Syndic 21: "4:20"

Waterways: "The Little Old Lady in the Woodstock T-Shirt," and first republished in the chapbook *All Our Fare-Thee-Wells*, Finishing Line Press, 2020

Contents

PART II—OUTSIDE THE WILD WEED DISPENSARY

PART I—REEFER MADNESS

4:20

I once asked our nephew
what those numbers meant,
assuming maybe a reference
to the Bible: smiting Amalekites,
the Song of Solomon,
witches burned or stoned to death,
women taken in adultery—
but never men—in one
sacred book or another.

He informed me it was the exact
time of day some California
high school kids fired up joints
and grooved to the Grateful Dead.

A relief, since I'd also feared
4:20 might be a reference
to Hitler's birthday: April 20th,
something kids thought cool,
Nazi salutes and goose-stepping
jokes their idiot parents wouldn't get,
not to mention the horrors
perpetrated on Hitler's birthday
at Columbine High School,
five miles down the road
from our Denver home.

A woman I knew went into labor
late one April 19th; she ordered
her doctor to perform a Caesarean.

"I will not have my son
born on that monster's birthday!"
the memory of the numbers
burned into her parents' arms
still a hot-blue flame.

The First Night I Tried Weed: Brooklyn College

One night of aimless driving,
I ran into Mark, the class hippie.
He held up a joint, as if Lady Liberty's
torch. In high school, it was gospel
that one "puff" would turn us
into groveling heroin addicts.

But now, in commuter college,
curiosity won. In his attic room,
Mark toked up and handed me the joint,
my lungs a forest fire; a second drag
ended in Keats's tubercular spasms.
By the third, I felt smoke mist down,
though still nothing, even with the trippy
guitar solo from "Dear Mr. Fantasy"
sizzling the stereo's speakers.
An hour later, sober as a mortician,
I thanked Mark and left, shaking
my head over what the big deal was.

My parents' Ford a brontosaurus,
my knuckles full-moon-white
to maneuver into a street narrow
as one of the alleys in Dickens' London,
footpads with truncheons blocking
both exits; somehow, I drove home
without smashing into a telephone pole,
and wheezed up the Matterhorn
to my parents' second floor apartment.

Giggling at a joke only I could get,
I fell into bed, the room a tilting merry-
go-round in a Hitchcock mystery,
but no desperation, thank God,
to shoot smack.

Druggie Songs

We smirked to quote the druggie lyrics
in "White Rabbit," the flute hypnotic
as a swami summoning a cobra,

or in "Lucy in the Sky," the acid reference
inescapable, the trippy melody taunting
anyone over thirty to figure out

what the song was about.
If music wouldn't save the world,
it was at least our secret code

against parents straight and dull as rulers,
speakers exploding with psychedelic decibels.
Those lyrics, our sacred texts, deeper

than Milton, Homer, Shakespeare,
the Bible, the sum of all knowledge,
all wisdom, the highest—pardon the pun—

of high poetry.
Well, we were young, and believed
we'd invented sex and drugs.

Mantras

Back in pot-head college days,
when I was afraid that what little
was left of my mind was clouding out
of my nose and mouth, and ripping
up my lungs like a roto-tiller,

I tried meditation: warned never,
under any circumstances, to divulge
my mantra to another soul—
more secret than the plans for D-Day;
I should concentrate on that holy phrase:
a formula to save the world. All I saw
were Aline Tannenbaum's breasts
in the Lotos Position.

Still dreaming of her, still repeating
the mantra of her perfection, I'd fall
asleep, wake in the morning, spending
as many hours in a slumber deep
as a sounding whale, as I would've
had I smoked a joint or twelve
while swaying in a haze to the Dead.

The last time, I realized too late
I hadn't studied for a mid-term;
crammed frantically. In class:
Aline leaned over her exam paper,
a glimpse of a Paradise
that nirvana couldn't possibly
begin to compete with.

The Lid

One night, six of us smoked
a lid of grass: an ounce.
We were young, immortal, stupid.

We played the Beatles'
White Album, over and over,
"Helter-Skelter" blasting away,

its hortator-insistent beat
smashing from speakers, friends
confiding I was twitching

like a frog zapped by electrodes:
"Epileptic seizure!" they gasped,
half terrified, half in awe.

God knows how many brain cells
I tossed away that night.
I declare now that if not

for that weed orgy,
I might've rivaled Keats.
Well, at least I have enough

gray matter left to make dumb jokes.

Mixed Messages

Signs all over the old Fillmore East
warned it was illegal to smoke weed:
Rock impresario Bill Graham covering
his ass, if the concert venue—a former
burlesque house—were ever raided.

You had to truck past the concession stand
before you could sit or dance in the aisles.
And what was it stocked with? Healthy
veggie burritos? Bracing chili bowls
on winter nights? Dried fruit for fiber-health?

Nah, nudge-nudge, wink-wink boxes of Oreos,
brownies, chocolate chip and oatmeal raisin cookies,
Häagen Dazs ice cream, and every variety
of chocolate carb you could dream of,
to stave off pot-propelled munchie attacks.

So yeah, a mixed signal, or capitalist hypocrisy,
when the grass cloud settled around the heads
of dancing, twirling revelers: a fog thicker
than 19th century London, than the toxic
steel-mill haze of 1950s Pittsburgh,

and a lot more likely to make you smile.

Smoking Dope Outside the Keats Museum: Hampstead Heath

Bud and I snuck onto the lawn—
maybe beside the very tree
where Keats had heard
his immortal nightingale—
and shared a joint,
our wives still inside.

Into our second round of tokes
when we saw the surveillance camera,
installed to record vandals and thieves,
our photos transmitted to Scotland Yard,
as Bud hid the roach.

"What have you two been doing?"
Beth demanded, sniffing the air
like the golden retrievers
she adored as a kid.

"For your information,"
El rebuked, "The Sixties
have been over for a decade,
and this is disrespectful to Keats,"
here she stared as pointedly
as an antique letter opener:
"His lungs crumbling
like the cloth wrapped around
a three-thousand-year-old mummy."

We shrugged: kids breaking
a picture window, promising restitution.
But whether it was the weed

or the museum or the time of year,
I heard someone softly chanting,
"Thou still unravished bride
of quietness," with the barest echo
of knowing laughter.

I Am So Stoned

Obligatory as rolling and passing
around joints, that every five minutes of so,
while "White Rabbit" or other druggie
anthems throbbed from the speakers,

it was someone's duty to declare
how wrecked they were: testimony
to our coolness and the potency
of the grass, thus, another kudo

to whoever had scored it.
It was as if announcing the height—
or depth—of our altered reality
was a mark of existential significance:

not enough to feel the top of our heads
about to zoom off into outer space,
to do loop-the-loop ellipses around
the Dead's "Dark Star,"

that twenty-three-minute trippy
music of the spheres: we weren't really
high until we announced
how very stoned we were.

Rolling Joints

I'd line up two Zig-Zag papers,
lick the edges, sprinkle on
a Goldilocks of weed,
then roll up the joint,
giving it my best shot,
but never able to get it tight
and neat as a Marlboro,
unlike some, who could roll
like Bogart in *The Big Sleep*.

From a childhood accident,
my right hand had less feeling
than an algae-covered rock.
One guy at a party called me
a spazz, seeing my two fumble-
fingered attempts before I got it right.
When I turned my wrist over
the raised scar—big as a bullfrog,
the livid pink of healed third-
degree burns—turned him gray,

before I passed him the joint,
and we communed
with the god of smoke,
the god of giggles,
the god who forgives.

Grandma Isabel Walks Along the Railroad Tracks, Rural Texas

Mornings, she walked with a sack
along the freight train line beyond
your West Texas town; returning,
she'd sit in her parlor window rocker
and roll cigarettes, fingers deft
as soldiers on the Western Front.

Then, she'd hum and smile to herself,
and maybe knit, or "Amen" to her Bible,
or just enjoy the sunlight on her face.

You were too young to really care
what she gathered, maybe something
to cook for dinner: your mother
too exhausted from her warehouse job
to sweat over a stove in the evening,
your father long gone to Dallas,
Houston, New Orleans, or wherever
charming hellers disappear to.

Years later, the revelation,
while passing a joint, that "Meemaw"
had been smoking dope.

"Jesus," you slapped your knee,
"Of course!" The logic irrefutable,
at least to our altered realities, dancing
to the music we—and maybe
your Meemaw—had heard.

Jimi: 1974

Spelling his name like Hendrix's,
he owned the neighborhood head shop:
incense a Hindu temple, display cases
of rolling papers, hash pipes, bongs, hookahs,
Indian blouses, serapes and ponchos;
posters of Hendrix, Dylan, Otis Redding.

He was possessed by the original Jimi's
riffs snaking from the PA system; me?
obsessed by the Dead; every now and then,
we'd part the bead curtains to where
he and Delores cooked, ate, and made love;
we'd toke up, Delores packing weed
into Ziploc bags, the shop more or less a front.

When I left for grad school Out West,
Jimi and I hugged, and when I returned
for Christmas break with Beth, whom I'd marry
and love forever, I stopped in to introduce her.

"Bob!" his bear hug levitated me,
and gently shook Beth's flute-playing hand.
"Man," he confided, "you left at the right time,"
and catalogued the shootings, the shop owners
robbed, the one murdered, and opened the drawer
under his cash register: a shiny-deadly pistol.

"Delores left, Man, couldn't take the bad vibes,"
he shrugged; neither Beth nor I able not to see
the hidden pistol, summers of love over.

Frankie and the Hash Genie

Some genies are better left in bottles,
like that hash I brought to Frankie's,
back when it was our civic duty
to turn on friends. I should've known,
when he asked me to hide his Bowie blade
and service revolver. Still, we passed
the pipe, then Frankie remarked,

"Check out the guy outside my front door."

"Frankie" I assured, "nobody's there."

"Please."

Of course, no one, so we smoked some more;
a minute later, Frankie's laughter startled
the darting cockroaches. High spirits contagious,
I joined in, then asked, "What's so funny?"

"If that guy behind the door could see me now,
he'd say, 'Man, you are so freaking stoned!'"

That's when I should've insisted, "Enough,"
but back then, too much was almost enough;
when I left, Frankie asked for the unsmoked chunk.

At work, he muttered he'd sat all night in his tub,
shower water finally making that staring man
disappear: a childhood priest who'd beat him
after confession, or someone dead from the War.

It's in the Bag

One night of wandering Brooklyn,
we found a brown paper bag
that looked like it was still stuffed
with someone's sandwich and apple,
and like Alice, we opened it.

"Holy shit," Ron breathed, "coke!"

"You sure?" I demanded, half curious,
half terrified, though this was at least
a decade before the great b-baller,
Len Bias, died from his first snort.

Ron licked a fingertip, nodded,
arranged little lines of dynamite
down the back of his hand,
and nodded, so again like Alice, I did.

Don't ask me how, but I was back
at my apartment, the energy
of Superman, to clean the place
three times. Still flying, I fixed meals
for the week, singing along
like the Seven Dwarfs,
then murmuring,

"Man, I could do this every day."
Luckily the bag was still with Ron.

Angel Dust

Back then, we'd have smoked anything,
even ground up dog turds, if we were told
it packed a hallucinogenic punch.
So horse tranquilizer by a psychedelic name?
Hell yeah! Idiots that we were, that I was.

I did it twice: once in two friends' East Village
apartment, where everyone gathered took turns
on the swing screwed into the living room ceiling:
a couple of hits, and I was flying at 35,000 thousand feet,
with total visibility of all that is, was, and would be.

The high so high, we tried it the next weekend;
and went to see *Fellini Satyricon;* during that sea
battle scene, with its ant's-eye-view of banks of oars
building to ramming speed, claustrophobia hit me
like a baseball bat, and I ran into the night,
but too frightened to cross the street
to the subway entrance, cars and taxis
whizzing past, daring me to step into the gutter.

Worse

I did psychedelics four times:
each trip worse than the one before;
well, I was young and stupid,
and it was the Sixties, our patriotic
duty to try as many drugs as possible.
The last time, a night in a sprawling house
in the Catskills; perfect, we thought,
and downed the dried mushrooms
with lemonade, to kill the taste
of the psychotropic poison.

We waited and waited and waited,
and were about to snort, "Fuhgeddaboutit,"
when those savage little buttons
kicked in like the boots of biker gangs.

Maddie still won't talk about what she saw,
but for me, two giant, smashing ball bearings,
the universe tearing itself apart,
and above that crashing, a voice
commanding me to abandon all hope,
for I was truly in Hell. Hours and hours
for the thunder and terror to subside,
and I could breathe again.

But Maddie couldn't. Nothing in the house
to calm her, so we sat in a diner
and I poured tea into her, tea even hotter
than her tears that streamed acid gullies
down her face.

Finally we staggered into an emergency room,
the resident, Maddie swore, a green homunculus
who'd waddled off a UFO; she grabbed
my hand and we ran out.

When at last we were seeing and hearing
nothing but New York City traffic,
we swore reality was strange and terrible enough:
war a demon that might swallow the world.

Stems and Seeds

The residue at the bottom
of a bag of grass we smoked
only if too lazy to leave the house
to score something with more
of a bang, especially if a storm
was tropical-rainforest cascading:

like the time I watched *Rain:*
Joan Crawford's cigarette smoke
drifting through her Malaysian hut's
bead curtain, one leg's black fishnet
stocking and stiletto heel erotically
arched through that flimsy threshold:

irresistible to the minister
who'd railed against her character,
a prostitute trying to reform.
He fell harder for her than angels
tossed from Heaven or a horny
young man watching
on a lonely Friday night.

I rolled stems and seeds into a joint;
those dregs not nearly the high
of Crawford's gams:
as our World War II
hero-dads used to wolf whistle.

Thursday Night Card Games

We played at my apartment,
overrun by more roaches
than the number of chips
Stu amassed each week:
with his memory more accurate
than an elephant reliving its past lives,
and a talent—perfect for the bar
he aspired to—for grabbing
any advantage he could.

So while the rest of us indulged in
a bit of the herb, he pretended
to draw the dope into his lungs,
his head clear as a glass of water
set before a hanging judge.

While we roared hilarity and testified
every five minutes how wrecked we were,
Stu played his hands quietly,
competently, the cards staring at
the rest of us as if moles ready to run away,
in the Queen of Hearts' cricket matches.

Still, Stu treated to midnight breakfasts
and a dissection of our every bad bet.

Hash Ash

We were sitting around my apartment:
smoking dope, scarfing Oreos and Cokes,
playing poker, when one of the guys, Dave?
The Stus? Jack? Harve? Me? came out with,

"This pot's so good, it's more like hash ash."

Utter nonsense that broke us up so hard,
both Stus fell off their chairs,
poker chips flying like flocks of swallows.

Coke fizz geysered from our noses,
the laughing jag finally ended in coughing
fits so loud they could've scared the ghosts
that haunted the deserted upper floors
of the brownstone where I cringed
from all-night bumps and moans.

"Hash ash," we repeated, at regular intervals
that night, and for months, and even now,
when Beth and I meet Dave, we'll ask,

"What the hell's 'hash ash?'"

No answer, but we'll tremble into giggle fits:
maybe just that we were young, all things possible,
wonderful, after we'd dodged Vietnam
and just wanted to get high and laugh,
before sober adult life set in.

The Drug Unit—Schermerhorn Center, New York City Department of Social Services

They were the caseworkers
who made sure junkies got into rehab
and stayed as clean as scalding showers,
that they got jobs, and didn't get fired,
which happened all too frequently.

But the temptation was hypnotic:
four of the caseworkers were mesmerized
by heroin's hooded cobra.
Only Carolyn resisted: the woman
you'd buy a lid from, if she knew you.

The others? Simon and Rick lost
their jobs in a skag fog, went on welfare.
Marilyn turned tricks, did time, got clean
and worked in a halfway house.

And Peter? Best not to ask about Peter.

Carolyn? She left Social Services
and went into teaching, swore
she'd never do or sell grass again,
claimed she didn't miss it, though
she never missed our Friday night
pot parties, her eyes prancing
at the air heavy with weed.

The Pause That Refreshes: Schermerhorn Center

Christmas Eve, 3 PM, so Alicia and a couple
of her co-workers strolled into the stairwell
and shared a few tokes. When they emerged,
eyes rolling like marbles, other caseworkers
had hung red and green bunting and festive
balloons, everyone impatient for the day
to end and the holiday party to begin.

Alicia sat as if she'd been shoved down,
bleary-headed, by a hostage taker.
When the pop went off, she screamed,

"Bomb! Bomb!"

Forget sweet reason, in those days
of Weathermen, IRA gunmen, Panthers
and cops we all knew were bloodthirsty pigs.

No one heard Hal plead it was a burst balloon.
Caseworkers, secretaries, and supervisors
stampeded into the street, Alicia wobbly legged,
as if she'd been sick on a freighter in rough seas.

"It's a miracle we're all alive," she gasped,
though when she heard Hal trying to convince
everyone struggling into their winter coats,

"It was just a burst balloon," she shot him a sneer
that could've knocked Hal to the pavement,

and demanded, "Are you nuts, or a damned terrorist?"

Grateful

I'm grateful I dread needles,
never tempted to shoot heroin:
at Dr. Avin's office when I was five:
one look at the syringe—longer
than a sabre toothed tiger's fang—
and it was almost a Marx Brothers routine:
poor Dr. Avin, no longer in storming-Omaha
Beach-shape, chased me around his office,
while I howled in an agony of terror
before he jabbed the needle in, gloating,

"Serves you right, you little bastard,"
which, he never said, but probably thought,
while my mother—that gorgeous traitor—
cut me off like a mustang cornered
by lasso-tossing cowhands in TV Westerns.

But I'm not as bad as my buddy Bill;
when we worked at the Department
of Social Services, we were told
if we gave blood that morning, we'd get
the rest of the day off: for movies,
or to smoke dope in the park, or whatever.

Sighting the syringe about to go into my arm,
Bill kissed the floor harder than if tagged
by an Ali uppercut, while I cringed, flexed
my fist, and succeeded in not shrieking,

though maybe a mini-shot of smack,
this once, might've eased my panic.

Mickey

By the time I met Mickey—
renting a room in a friend's apartment—
he was more or less addicted only
to grass, starting in the bathroom
before he went to work repairing
guitars in a neighborhood shop.

His cough carried like a hurricane,
pulling smoke in deep as the Marianas Trench.
At work, he was never without a joint,
like a chain-smoking film-noir detective.

Watching TV, Mickey toked
while he noodled away on an old Martin,
sang Dylan, Baez, the Dead,
and bragged he'd played in a band
that almost, almost went national.

When he jammed at my "Fare-
Thee-Well to New York" party,
he'd come in too early, too late, not at all,
and stormed out, his scuffed boots
shuddering the splintered floor.

Two days later, Mickey's eyelids were heavy
as flooding levee sandbags; he mumbled,
when he talked at all, and a day after that,
when he disappeared, he took the wad
of bills Laurie had hidden in a drawer,
but left his guitar, smashed to pieces.

The Little Old Lady in the Woodstock T-Shirt

I spot her in the Safeway parking lot,
at least 80 and hanging onto her shopping cart
as if teetering with vertigo at a cliff's edge,
her cane resting on the cart's handle.

On her T-shirt, the Woodstock symbol:
birds trilling on a guitar's frets,
Love and Peace in the grass-aromatic air,
while her cart totters with the blind
staggers to her Bug that she trembles open.

"Can I help you, Ma'am?" I ask,
as she struggles to lift her shopping bag
as if a barbell, and drops the dead weight
into the back seat.

She stares at me, as if afraid
I'll hit her over the head for her purse
she grips like a lifeline, which maybe it is:
with all her money, I.D., and credit cards.

She looks at me again, notes my beard,
what's left of my hair gathered in a ponytail,
sees my Jerry Garcia T-shirt, and demands,

"Wanna score some righteous shit?
If not, get the fuck outta my face."

The Weed Tree

Its branches majestic
at the edge of Washington Park,
across from Denver's South High.
Kids gathered under its branches
and passed joints for the strength—
or oblivion—to sit through classes.

When we'd walk the park's perimeter,
Beth and I stopped, and I'd breathe
as if standing, gasping on Mount Evans,
sucking in a contact high.

Mostly it was reefered-up hoodied boys
but once two girls joined them, maybe
from Pakistan, desperate to fit into America,
innocent of how nasty teenagers could be.

The girls tossed off their veils, rolled up
the sleeves and the hems of their long,
shimmering dresses, tired of being treated
as if they'd break apart like crystal,

while the boys nudged each other,
smirked, and winked, and Beth and I
wondered, worried, if we'd have
to wade in to protect those girls' honor.

Then they all ambled to the entrance,
and we strolled up the park's first hill,
me floating a bit, pointing out to Beth,
the red-tailed hawk making lazy, lovely,

merciless circles above the lake.

Skunk Hour

Whenever we walk to our car,
that skunk-stink, Beth calls it;
for me, the aroma of the kids
next door smoking righteous weed.
I'll stop a moment and breathe
as deeply as I would spruce-fresh air
after a hike to a mountain waterfall.

If I'm with Beth, I'll make it quick,
her nose wrinkled up, as if a polecat
really had let loose. Alone, I'll stare
at their open window, tempted to bum
a toke or twelve, Beth putting her foot
down, about dope in the house,

though I keep a pinch or two, waiting
for an afternoon when Beth's at school,
to indulge a bit, unlike these kids
who seem to smoke twenty hours a day,
their lungs must look like cheese cloth,
though I have to admire their stamina

and that they can still get to work
or attend the college down the hill,
when my knees used to turn to just-
from-the-boiling-pot noodles,
my brains a snow drift
I couldn't possibly slog through.

The Guinness Record for Pot Smoking

Maybe he's going
for a Guinness record,
since even in my foggiest
60s pot smoking days,
I didn't have his stamina.

Every time we walk to our car,
that lovely skunk stink hits us
through his open window.
Beth's eyes tear; I try to breathe
a contact-aperitif before we drive off
on errands or out to dinner.

Now that pot's legal and a dispensary's
just down the block, the temptation's
almost as overwhelming as crisping bacon:
another forbidden pleasure
on my gout induced red-meat-taboo diet:

except Beth would kill me
if I started again, my lungs tattered
gauze for years, as, I imagine, the lungs
of our next-door-neighbor will soon be,
smoke wafting as if from a dry ice machine.

Come to think of it, I've not seen him
leave his house for weeks, like I was:
a mole burrowing into a haze of weed,
acid rock, Oreos, and loneliness.

At least he's not paralyzed
by the paranoia that possessed me,
knowing that at any moment,
cops could smash down
my drug saturated door.

Got Pot?

Ever since weed's been legal here,
I'm waiting for billboards showing
drifting smoke and the caption,

"Got Pot?"

like the ones with white smudges
across upper lips, that ask,

"Got milk?"

So far, nope; still, I'm hopeful,
though my dope smoking days are over:
one toke and I'll cough for hours;
as for edibles, who knows how much
to bite off for a hit that won't send me
jumping off tall buildings: suicidal Superman.

And where's the ritual in scarfing down
brownies, chocolate chip cookies, Tootsie Rolls,
or a drop of hash oil on a slice of ciabatta,
compared to the almost sacred communion
of passing around joints or pipes?

Though if billboards showed actors
with a glass of milk, a half-eaten chocolate-
something, and spacy, wink-wink smiles:
now *that* would be supremely hip, utterly ironic.

AAA and the AA

A friend half jokes he'll give up
his driver's license and AAA membership,
to concentrate on drinking: the country
flapping away on Trump's vampire-bat wings.

"A liquor store I know will deliver,
and so will the local supermarket,
so no need to leave the house and risk
being the victim of an alt-right's road rage.

"Then again," he quips, "at my age,
I should cut back on the booze
and smoke dope, now that it's legal here;
can't make me any dumber than I feel:

"So sure the Orange Nightmare
didn't have a chance. Besides, weed
might help me laugh through the next
how many years of Trump's reign of terror."

"So maybe I'll try drink *and* dope,
to get me through."
What with the dispensary down the block,
and the liquor store just around the corner,

I'm ready to try the same experiment.

Now That It's Legal

If I'm honest, now that it's legal
here in Colorado, pot isn't
as much risky fun anymore,
as, for instance, that time,
I brought a lid to two friends.

I wore a tie and corduroy sports coat,
though my stab at respectability
was ruined by black Converse sneakers
and a pair of jeans that might've
been worn by John the Baptist,
as the old joke went,
since they were so hole-y.

I strolled the gauntlet of two beat cops
while hiding the ounce in a day pack
and staring at the translation of *The Inferno*
in my hands, and sweated a rain forest,
but somehow reached their apartment
safely as a spy with top secret instructions.

After I exchanged the lid for cash;
we smoked some, and smoked
some more, and some more.

I never got so happy-high in my life,
which might've had as much to do
with outsmarting The Law
as with the quality of the weed.

My Favorite Aromas

Trouble falling asleep last night,
I started naming my favorite aromas:
a really good navel orange,
the blending of sweet and acid
like a love nip's sweet pain and pleasure;
a chunk of dark chocolate thick
enough to linger on the tongue
like the best memory of childhood;
bacon, of course, the delicious mingling
of salt and sweet, to make me wonder
why I'd waited so long to try it,
though taboo in our kosher apartment.

Then there's the aroma no one else
in the world would agree with,
except my buddy Dave, here in Denver:
that skunky fragrance of potent weed
I've been sniffing ever since the herb
was legalized in our enlightened state.
I'll stroll to the mailbox and pass
some kids from the college exhaling
that divine stench; I'll breathe deep,
the aroma heady as the pastrami
I loved as a kid, the sandwich
I'd demand for that one last meal
before I won't be able to smell
anything, ever again.

Why I Don't Smoke Pot Anymore

Or rarely: with old friends
on a night of good conversation,
good food, heartfelt singing;
I'll take a toke or two, and cough
and cough, to my wife's worried glares.

And despite everyone saying
pot's head-smashing stronger
than when I'd score an ounce
every few weeks, and kick back
and hear the music of the spheres
or laugh my *tuchus* off with friends
over the greatest jokes and stories
ever, or never, told—Nothing:

No munchies, no everything
more intense, more mellow,
no flashing lights and colors,
like when I hallucinated
emerald sevens and ruby
horse heads flashing on the wall,
my own trip-the-light
fantastic lightshow.

Now That Colorado

Now that Colorado's legalized marijuana,
its skunky aroma is everywhere.
Like this morning, when I drove my wife
and a visiting research colleague of hers
to the college, for an early business breakfast,
the highway was a humidor of weed.
And later, when I pulled into our driveway,
from our next-door neighbor's late-spring
open-window, the Pepe-Le-Pew bouquet.

Something bothers me about this, not
that the whole state's going all Lotus on me,
thus ripe for the Islamic and Mexican invasions
certain politicians preach will keep America
from being great again, but that any schmuck
with enough money can buy excellent pot,
as if selecting a cigar or bottle of wine.

In my day—geezer that I am—it took
some discernment to score primo weed,
and always the fear the dealer was a narc,
or if you sweated sauntering past beat cops,
they'd stop you faster than Killer Kowalski's
professional-wrestler Atomic-Drop-Kick move.

And now the Girl Scouts will sell cookies
outside pot shops! I ask you, is nothing sacred?

PART II—OUTSIDE THE WILD WEED DISPENSARY

"The Girl Scouts of Colorado have decided it's now cool to peddle their baked goods outside marijuana dispensaries."

—The Denver Post

Melvin Dickson, the Girl Scouts, and Pot Shops

The little dolls wear Cheshire Cat smiles:
drug dealers in training, sirening how perfect
a combo weed, Thin Mints, Lemonades, or Trios
would make: the instant munchie cure.

But now it's legal, not as much fun
as scoring from a neighborhood dealer,
his kitchen delicious with weed-stink,
then on the look-out for cops dying to bust
a guy trying to take the edge off his week.

I remember once, when I brought a lid
to a friend in need, I wore my sports jacket,
and carried the dope in a satchel
when I walked past a black-and-white.
Afterwards, a rush like cheating death.

Now, smiling pre-teen angels offer me
boxes of cookies. I dart inside, stroll out
with a paper bag full of stuff guaranteed
to blow away the top of my skull,
and all of it legal as sitting at a hotel bar.

So why do I feel like a pusher contributing
to the delinquency of minors? Though,
more likely, they're the Lorelei tempting me.

Wilhelmina Larsen with Her Daughter, Outside the Wild Weed Dispensary

Inspired by today's location
for selling Girl Scout cookies,
I stopped off yesterday
at the Wild Weed for a joint.

I used to smoke with Ron,
before love and marriage
became a baby carriage,
and things got stinky as bad grass,
what with that Claire he fell for
hard as a dropped anvil;
Ron so deep into fuckland,
he forgot he had a daughter
he's supposed to love more than life.

That joint helped me forget him,
made me ravenous, so I cracked open
a box: those Lemonades yummy.

Now in front of the dispensary,
I've a craving for the smoking hair
of the dog, so I tell Melissa to make sure
no one touches the cigar box, and run inside
for an ounce and some Zig-Zags.

After we count the take tonight,
and I tuck Melissa in with her Little Pony,
Mama's gonna have a fine ole time;
too bad no one to share the high with.

Melissa Larsen, Age Ten, Girl Scout

Mommy doesn't know I saw her smoking
that stinky cigarette that smells even worse
than the real ones Daddy's new friend
Claire smokes, when he has me over,
which isn't often. I hate her, and she doesn't
like me one bit, except when Daddy's
in the room; then she's my best friend.

She thinks I'm a moron, like Mommy does,
running into the store just now, to buy
more marijuana for when I'm asleep tonight,
telling me to make sure people pay for their cookies.

Tiffany's older brother tried to get us to smoke,
but our teacher warned we'd become maniacs
and have to live in straitjackets, like forever.
Tiff looked like she wanted to, so I ordered
Teddy out of her room; he shrugged
the sexiest shrug ever and called out,

"Let me know when you lovely ladies
change your pretty little minds,"
so I wanted to faint the way Grandma did
for the Beatles, and almost took a puff.

I just hope I won't have to call 911 tonight,
if Mommy goes into a coma: bad enough
Daddy's acting like a teenager, but even
Mommy's not Mommy anymore.

Melissa Larsen: Part II

I wish Mommy would hurry up
and buy what she thinks
I don't know what she's buying.
People outside are weird:
one man looks like the Big Bad Wolf
with his beard and eyes sharp as teeth;
the college kids tease I'm a pusher,
and a boy and his girlfriend looked
over the different flavors, touching
every single one, high as the plane
Mommy and I took to Grandma's
for Christmas; at least they bought
a couple of boxes.

What's taking Mommy so long?
College kids look like they'd steal
some boxes, like in the heist movies
Daddy watches with bitchy Claire,
forgetting I'm in the room, their mouths
like bathroom-plunger sucking cups
and grabbing each other: my tummy
squishing like the world's ickiest thing.

Finally! But Mommy's smiling
like she's already smoked
that awful stuff that bulges her purse
like the nasty chewing-tobacco
baseball players spit during the games
Daddy watches, and me too,
if I want him to myself, Claire out shopping.

Gary Auger, Proprietor of the Wild Weed
Dispensary

I was skeptical, letting kids sell cookies
right outside, their munchies chomping
into my edible trade. But a win-win
for me and the Scouts, and just now,
the mom of one girl bought a lid,
wanting a hummingbird buzz
not something to knock her on her ass.

Damn fine-looking woman, too,
surprising she had a ten-year-old,
plus she came on to me
when I showed her various blends,
letting her sniff like fine perfumes
or testing wines for their nose.

She put her hand on my wrist
to steady herself, and let it linger,
her fingers warm as if she'd held
a mug of tea, when she bent forward
and snorted deep as if doing a line.

She wasn't wearing a wedding band,
but you could see she had, recently,
so after she stashed the lid in her purse,
I asked if she'd like to go for coffee
sometime; she smiled and handed me her card.

In college, I was the geek of all geeks,
so I wonder: is it my newfound charm
or the aroma? Almost hallucinatory
when I open up every morning.

Ron Larsen Has Doubts About Letting His Daughter Sell Cookies

I won't say I'm getting even with Winnie
for taking the house, the assets I didn't hide,
and oh yeah, little Mellie's love, when I hooked
up with Hot Claire, but revenge is sweet.

When Winnie said Mellie's troop was selling
cookies in front of dispensaries, my turn
to be Mr. Moral, Winnie acting like I was a pig
for ditching her for a newer, sexier model.

"How do I know," I sounded holy as Billy Graham,
"Mellie won't get sucked into an evil weed vortex
and become a raving, frothing junkie?"

Winnie stared like I was the dumbest bastard
in the Rocky Mountains, though I'd spied her
ducking into that dispensary and flouncing out smug
as the Cheshire Cat and the Caterpillar's hookah.

"Maybe I'll sue for full custody," I smirked,
a bluff to get some of my hard-earned capital back,
since Sexy Claire thinks Mellie puts the stink-eye
on her, the kid cramping our style when she's here,
but anything to put the fear of divorce lawyers into Winnie.

"Say Claire, Hon" I call out, "pour us another glass
of that Cab; we already killed the first two bottles."

Leonard Millstein, Father of a Girl Scout: Outside the Wild Weed

I wish Marissa had chaperoned Emily,
but my wife's far too busy: an attorney
for a corporation that spews
more toxic waste than Chernobyl,
not a mere lawyer like me.

"Besides," she accuses,
"You hardly see Em, Mr. Public Defender,
springing criminals from prison,
which is where they belong."

As opposed to the patriots
she helps to ravage the planet?
"And," Marissa's final argument,
"you can score something for us
to chill with tonight."

Chill? Really? I'll get paranoid,
like always, and cough like a TB ward;
plus, I'm terrified of edibles: my buddy
Lenny ate a psychedelic Tootsie Roll
and hallucinated like a drooling vegetable
for ten not-so-straight hours.

Well, here I am with Em, trying not
to hover, Em sulking, to be stuck
with clueless dad. She'll rifle
our bedroom for the stash Marissa expects.
At least Em doesn't know the combination
to the wall safe where Mommy keeps the gun
I've been begging her to get rid of.

I'd accidentally forget to make the buy,
but Em keeps tugging at my sleeve.

Marissa Millstein Thinks of Her Husband Leonard

Easy to guilt Leonard into chaperoning
Emily's Girl Scout troop. I told him
I'm point woman on a crucial work project,
and accuse, "You never take an interest in Emily."

That part's almost true, but the big project?
Walter and I twined like a pair of anacondas.
The thought of it sends me into Fifty Shades
of lubricious anticipation: Leonard? I nod out
when he drones on about the losers he defends
who can't afford real attorneys.

The perv he got off on that capital charge?
You can't tell me he didn't do it, no matter
if Leonard "proved" with DNA and time stamps
that killer wasn't at the scene; just clever to cover
his tracks. An IQ of 78? You can fake that.

How long have Walter and I been doing it?
Let's just say my idealistic husband's clueless
as a bloodhound without a sense of smell.
If Leonard and Emmie beat me home,
I'll call to say I'm running late,
and bubble something cool to Emmie.

If he ever finds out, I'll spin it as pay-back
for his spending more time with his deadbeat
clients than with me. Then, I'll sue,
Walter an alpha divorce lawyer.

By the time he's finished with Len,
my ex'll be out on the street, cup in hand.
And I used to think him cute as a puppy.

Emily Millstein, Selling Cookies Outside the Wild Weed

Mommy has a new friend,
and Daddy's so, like, clueless,
I hate her friend, hate her even more,
for fooling Daddy. I shake at night,
that she'll leave us for him.

And I hate it that I'm so mean to Daddy,
because he can't see what's as plain
as the other cellphone Mommy keeps
in her attaché case; it'll break his heart
when she tells him, like a movie star
cursing a pesky photographer, she's leaving.
She'll want to take me, but I won't go.
I wish Daddy told her, "You're staying
with us, and that's that!"

I keep hoping, if maybe they smoked
marijuana together, they'll fall back in love,
like the hippies in old movies:
why I keep nagging Daddy to buy some.
People who leave this shop have silly grins;
they buy boxes of cookies, and tear into them
before they walk away or get into their cars,
like Girl Scout cookies are the best idea ever.

So maybe marijuana will help Mommy forget
about her new, stinky friend. I wanted
to poison him the one time I met him
and he smiled at me like the Big Bad Wolf,
and gave me a twenty-dollar bill,

and Mommy made me say, "Thank you,"
like I meant it, then told me to go play
down the block with one of my friends,
while she's like, playing with her new toy.

Rebecca Charters, High School Librarian and Leader of Girl Scout Troop 63

How things have changed
from when our venues
were in front of supermarkets,
movie theaters, mall entrances,
and churches.

Now? In front of the Wild Weed,
the girls in frenzies trying to score,
as likely as convincing some
of my high school students
to check out a book, their cellphones
telling them the meaning of life.

The library? A place to flirt,
not caring other kids are studying
or—heaven forbid—reading for fun.
When I ask them to be quiet, they mutter,

"What's your problem, man?"
either verbally lazy or letting me know
they know I'm married to Cecily,
as if that's a state secret.
Her love makes me wonder
why I gave Ted a first, let alone
a second and third chance.

"Melanie," I shout, "away from the door!"
She slinks off, a cheeky vixen-grin,
other girls cheering her brass to try.
And here comes Sally, thinking I'm asleep,
as if the owner would sell them a joint!

Lord, once this day is over, I'll need
a toke or twelve, a glass of Chardonnay,
and Cecily rubbing my back.

Franklin Ambrose, Single Father, Chaperoning His Girl Scout Daughter, Elise

When Andrea left, saying she needed
to find herself, like she'd lost a pair of pumps,
I had to be father and mother to Elise.
After she stopped crying, and I stopped
wanting to punch holes in walls, I enrolled her
in the Girl Scouts, other kids to pick up her spirits
like jacks in the game girls used to play.

Single mothers came out of the woodwork
with casseroles, cakes, and kindness, not
that I was interested, or just a little,
but it's so much effort, and Elise needs me
to be a full-time dad, so maybe when she goes
off to college I'll have a social life again.

I don't even keep grass around the house,
afraid Elise might find it, so it's kind of funny
to hang out in front of the Wild Weed Dispensary,
which reminds me of the old song,
"Wildwood Flower," we used to sing
an electric version of in our garage band:

How I met Andrea: taking in our set at a bar,
back in college. I thought myself the world's
luckiest guy when she sashayed over and told us
how good we were, her eyes licking me like ice cream,
while scissoring a finger through her long red hair,
standing with one leg pretzeled around the other
in that sexy way girls know they're driving you nuts.

I wanted to spend the rest of my life with her:
at least she left me Elise: good to see her laugh again,
with her friends, all of them teasing they want to grab
some grass, experts at yanking adults' chains.

Elise Ambrose, Girl Scout

Mommy left us, didn't say why, but obvious
she hated me, though Daddy says that's not true:
lying to save my feelings. But somehow,
a while ago, I stopped crying and Daddy stopped
wanting to hit things; well, what he really wanted
to hit was Mommy, but you can't do that anymore.
And when he enrolled me in the Girl Scouts,
it was like I had a hundred new friends, though
most were from my school, so I knew them already.

Daddy's discovered he can cook a lot better
than Mommy, who flung pots and pans
like they'd all dared shoot her the finger.
He works at his computer upstairs all day,
so he's always here, which makes me feel safer
than kids who let themselves in after school,
and pray no maniac's hiding in a closet,
to leap out and shoot them, like at schools
Daddy won't let me watch about on TV;
I tell him my school has drills for that.

Now, I wish he'd find a friend his own age;
I don't need him to take me everywhere with him,
that's what the Scouts are for. He needs
a nice lady to make him smile like he means it,
and isn't doing it to make me think he's okay.
When I ask him if he wants to go out sometime,
with someone, he pats my head like I'm a dog
doing tricks and tells me there's plenty of time.

"No there isn't," I want to shout back, "you're not
getting younger!" Thinking that makes me scared,
though I know Samantha's mother is all alone,
and while people buy boxes and boxes of cookies,
she's actually talking to Daddy and smiling!

Donnie Fowler, Boy Scout

It's not fair! Everyone loves
the Girl Scouts for their cookies.
And now they get to sell them
outside pot shops? They'll get
free samples, while I gotta steal
my older brother Neal's stash,
though the one time I smoked,
my lungs felt like a grizzly
was standing on them.

What do we get? A speech by Trump,
who, my dad says is a Russian spy.
I saw him on TV, and like other kids,
I cheered: Yeah, America First; Yeah,
Hillary's a crook; Yeah, lock her up!
And Man, did Mom smack me,
then started crying and asked Dad,

"What kind of monster did we raise?"

I cried too, not even knowing why
everyone's so angry at each other:
like Gramps, who says Dad's nothing
but an Islamist-Terrorist-Commie
and should be shot, though according
to Mom, Gramps never did like Dad
in the first place, called him,

"A low-life hippie drug fiend,"
when Mom and him started dating.

So the Girl Scouts get all the praise,
while we have to go on hikes,
and watch the President shout,

my teacher saying he sounds like Hitler,
though I'll be damned—darned—if I know
who he was, too embarrassed to ask.

Vicki Gleeson, Girl Scout

Brad, Mom's live-in boyfriend, yelled
loud as a dumb Transformer movie,
when we left to sell cookies,

"Score me some of that weed!"
He is so gross, and Mom so stupid
to fall for his smile and his guitar
playing in his band that really sucks.

If a boy lay on the couch and watched
TV all day, while spazzing out on his "axe,"
and bellowed for his dinner, I'd toss him
into the street faster than Kathy Reynolds
can run the 60-yard dash in P.E. class.

Mom drove and I sat with my arms wrapped
around my chest, to keep from screaming,

"It's me or him!" afraid she'd say,
"Get lost," since Mom's like that
with her strays, until they break
her heart and bank account.
Jesus, doesn't she ever learn?
I'll never let a boy hook up with me,
the ones at school just pimple piles!

At the pot shop, I jump out before Mom
kisses me like she doesn't know how mad I am.
She gets out too, to chaperone and score Brad
some weed that will stink up our house,
the two of them passing a pipe like Lakotas
at a peace powwow, and not dirty junkies.

Deidre Gleeson, Mother of Vicki

I know Vicki hates my new boyfriend Brad,
but which one hasn't she hated? Up to her,
I'd still be with her father, that deadbeat Cole,
who, if I'm honest, I still burn for.

Hell, if I'm really honest, every guy
I've ever been with has been a clone
of Cole's swaggering, "I don't give a shit
about anything except my cool, badass self."

Why am I so spastically attracted to outlaws,
or to losers who think they're outlaws,
guys in bands without a lick of talent
or drive, just the belief they'll make it

some day through no effort of their own?
I should listen to Vicki: eleven, but wise
and bitter as a radish, which makes me so sad,
like she's a forty-year old divorcee in a kid's body.

I should ditch that slug, Brad: at least three fathers
here who, I know for sure, are no longer married,
and all of them look pretty good, and act like real
fathers, which is more than Brad knows how to fake.

I could strike up a conversation and see where it goes,
and maybe, just maybe, get pleasantly surprised.

Brad Whittaker Waits at His Girl Friend's House

Damn, Deidre couldn't just drop off
her little bitch of a kid, score me
some grass and hightail it back here?
She has to chaperone the tiny twerpette,
who's always getting between me and Dee?

Hey, that rhymes, the hook for the song
I'm trying to compose for my band. Too bad
the kid doesn't live with her deadbeat dad.
It takes so much freakin' energy to pretend I care
about the brat; if she were to walk into traffic,
I'd shed a tear or two, for Dee's sake, but happy
on the inside, as a buzzard with a donkey carcass.

She never says nothing when I noodle classic
Dylan songs, or one of the new pieces for my band;
just sneers, rolls her eyes in fake boredom,
'cause she secretly knows I've got the chops
to make it big, and if the world was fair,
should've already, like when we sent
that demo tape to that New York producer
who probably stole our tunes and lyrics
for a skank-band he's promoting.

Dee won't be back 'til the little horror's
ready to come home, so we'll have to wait
'til she goes to bed before we can toke up,
get all loosey-goosey and have some fun.
I'm sick of her kid always coming first.
My life would've been a whole lot easier
if I'd fallen this hard for a single lady.
Better call and tell Dee to buy a pizza.

Samantha Garcia, Denver Girl Scout

It's okay Mom's talking to Elise's father;
she's been so sad since Daddy died;
even before, when he looked so old, so gray,
in so much pain, no strength to say anything,
though I knew what his eyes were begging,
and ran into the hall, to cry.

Still, it's only a year, and I see Daddy
everywhere: in our house, the backyard
weeding, mowing the lawn, taking care
of the roses he loved, though he'd fake threaten,
"You're in big trouble now, Sister,"
whenever a thorn stung him.

Thinking of that, I laugh, then cry;
he was so smart and handsome;
I'm afraid I'll forget his face, his voice,
his helping me with my homework,
'til he got too tired, in too much pain.

Now, I sell cookies in front of this pot shop,
with the other girls in my troop;
we smile at customers; I hand out boxes
and write down names for our mailing list,
Elise counts out change.

We glance at our parents, chatting, smiling.
Her dad looks like a nice man, though not Daddy,
but as long as Mom's happy, I can try too.

Margaret Baxter, Not Allowed to Participate

"I will not," Papa shouted, "have my daughter
tempted by this evil, anti-Jesus drug, and that's that!"
He makes it sound like the owner will hand us
free joints to get us hooked, or brownies so laced
with grass, one nibble will put us in straitjackets.
Or like, we'll tunnel under the Wild Weed's sidewalk
into the vault, and haul out giant plastic trash bags
of the stink-weed to sell with our Girl Scout cookies.

I roll my eyes at his Bible rants, refuse to beg
his and God's forgiveness, so he shouts I'm a demon
hurling straight to hell, his eyes so scary, I'm afraid
he'll kill me to save my soul, though Mama whispers
for me to run up to my room and lock the door.

As much as I love him, I'm starting to hate him;
I wish he hadn't visioned Jesus in his heart attack,
claiming the Lord told him it wasn't his time,
but to go back down and, "Prepare the way for Me
to cleanse My Kingdom," or something even nuttier.

Mama "Amens" but looks out for me though
pretty soon, we'll all be dressed in white robes,
and he'll make me stand on street corners with him,
shouting, "Repent!" when all I want is to hang out
with my friends and do what they're doing,
which, right now, is selling cookies in front of pot shops.

Mrs. Brenda Baxter

Darryl was always a bit kooky,
why I fell for him, but what I took
for goofiness before that heart attack
turned downright weird afterwards,
like changing his name to Jeremiah,
and ordering Maggie and me about
what we could and couldn't say and do;
heck, telling everyone they were hell bound
unless they repented.

Maggie was already in the Girl Scouts,
or he'd never have let her join,
but when she asked if she could help sell
cookies outside the Wild Weed Dispensary,
you'd think walking-dead meth heads
would be biting innocent girls into zombies.

For the sake of our marriage I went along with him,
but it hurt Maggie to be left out, afraid
other girls whispered her father was crazy.

If we try to escape him, Jeremiah will toss us into
a locked basement room to bring us to Jesus.
When he works himself into a Bible rant, I fear
another coronary, but lately, I almost don't care.

It's not like he didn't smoke dope back in the day:
arguing with his dad about it, who claimed grass
would turn him into a raving junkie,
the old man downing rye shots like orange juice.

Margaret Baxter Disobeys Her Father

I snuck out when he was praying,
hopped a bus to the Wild Weed,
where our troop was selling cookies,
but the scout leader asked,

"Maggie, where's your mom?
Wasn't she supposed to chaperone you,
and did she sign the release form?"

I lied that I'd forgotten the paper,
but Rebecca gave me the stink-eye,
so I got all hissy-fitty and whined
it'd waste so much time to get it,
and Mom was perfectly okay
with me being there: Rebecca figuring
I was safer with her than on the bus all alone,
with every perv in Denver riding the 12,
so she let me stay, and didn't call Mom
or Dad, though he'd have yelled
she's a sodomite, whatever that is.

The stench drifting out of the Wild Weed
is pukeful, but it's legal, though Daddy—
or Papa, as he now wants me to call him—
rants that "abortion, that abomination, is also legal!"

Like I'm old enough to have an abortion;
it's so yucky to think about being pregnant,
which I will never, ever be: the thought
of boys' slimy lips and wet tongues turns
my stomach into cold, squishy oatmeal.

But it's fun to be with my friends,
all of us joking about getting high,
and if Dad locks me in my room forever
when I get home, it'll be worth the escape.

Ruthie Morgan, Girl Scout

I've got to steal a joint for Gary,
who smirked when I told him
we'd be selling cookies outside
the Wild Weed,

"Make yourself useful," hinting
we could go steady if I did.
Maybe I can sneak in and the owner
will be in the back, so I can grab some,
though I feel like a fawning Irish setter.

But I said I'd score him some shit:
how my parents talk about pot,
so maybe I should search their drawers,
since if I don't bring Gary some,
he'll call me a skank.
Like all I'm good for is to give
him presents and fall down, too grateful
to say a word, when he shrugs,

"Hey thanks, man," like he did me a favor:
not worth talking to unless I let him cheat
off me on tests, or lend him my homework,
or worse, smile when he grabs my breasts
that are just starting to come in,
and Mom confiding about the icky blood.

I wish I was a boy and not have to think about it.
So on second thought, screw you, Gary.
You want some dope? Score your own!

Malcolm Sanders, Police Detective, with His Girl Scout Daughter

I bust pushers, and now my little angel's
selling cookies outside the Wild Weed,
almost makes me feel like an accessory.

My job was too much for Kelly's mother:
When we walked in from a Scout function,
we found her note, saying she couldn't take
the hours I had to put in, the danger.
She didn't mention the guy on the side;
you think cops don't have ways of finding out?
I fight the temptation to hunt them down, and,
well, best not to mention what "and" entails.

At least folks buying dope and cookies here
look harmless: no mosquito-bite track marks,
though I want to frisk them all, to make sure
no one's packing and starts firing
at innocent kids and parents when he lams out
with a sack heavier than a wrong-way Santa:
the grass business all cash, unless the Feds
make it legal, which, with this president
and AG, I don't see happening, thank God.

Still, it's good Kelly's hanging out with her friends,
and learning arithmetic the old-fashioned way,
by making accurate change, how I learned
at my dad's candy store, after school.

Kelly Sanders, Girl Scout

Mommy left a note on the kitchen table
that she couldn't take Daddy's police hours
or that every time he left for work he might
not come home. What she was really saying:
she was tired of loving me, when she'd found
someone her own age to have fun with.

Staring at that note, Daddy hugged me, too hard,
and swore nothing bad would ever happen.
Bad stuff always happens; like when I'd listen
from the top of the stairs when Daddy got home late
and Mommy'd sob she'd been so worried,
her breath smelly with wine.

Mrs. Gillespie, the lady who knits and watches me
when I get home from school, always coos,

"Don't fret, honey, he'll be in right on time."

He's never on time, and Mrs. Gillespie sighs,
annoyed she can't be with her own family,
so I'll cook hamburgers and microwave French fries,
with maybe some lettuce that's not too wilted,
and she and I will eat, running out of things to say;
we'll wait and wait, and I'll bite my lip in worry,
while she taps her toe and makes knitting mistakes,
until Daddy's finally home, hardly the strength
to thank Mrs. Gillespie and fork food in.
At least he doesn't take down the scotch bottle.

Making cookie-change now, I keep hoping
Mommy'll walk up, and give me a hug,
then kiss Daddy: loving us both, again.

Fiona Terry, Girl Scout

Mom shoved me into the Girl Scouts;
we pledge allegiance "like a bunch of fascists,"
according to Dad, who teaches at the university
and tells me all about World War II,
so I know what's really going on in the world,
while Mom goes all stink-eye that I'm growing
up way too fast. You can't grow up fast enough,
not with what's happening to the country.
Just ask Dad.

I hang with girls who barely talk to me at school,
when I'd rather be reading and not have to hear
their oil-spill gushing about kissing and making out.

Now, the super dumbest thing: selling cookies,
which taste good only if you're stoned.
President Lincoln was wrong: you *can* fool
enough people enough of the time to sell them
just about any piece of crap you want.

At least Mom's not asking if I'm having fun.
Of course I'm not: other girls call me "Spazz,"
make remarks about my eyeglasses, which work:
a lot more important than "sexy."

"Sexy?" At our age? They're brain-dead,
to prance and pout for dirty-minded little boys.
Feminism's what we should be selling,
not pimping cookies outside a pot shop.

Mom swore if I didn't like it, I could quit
in a year: two months to go! Amazing,

she loved the Scouts; little Storm Troopers,
with these uniforms and salutes
and group activities you can't skip.

Girl Scouts? Hitler's
Youth League's more like it!

Toni McLemore, Girl Scout

My head all but explodes
when girls in my Troop tell me
they're "Keeping it real!"
and everything's "Dope,"
when Mom and Dad want me
to talk like a combination of
Wonder Bread, Yale,
and *The New York Times.*

Now in front of this pot shop,
the girls all gasp, "What's it like?"
assuming I popped out toking away:
the Little Black Engine That Could.
The only girl I like is Fiona:
her head, like mine, always in books,
her glasses thicker than hockey pucks.

"Don't hang with her," girls warn.
"She's like, so uncool!"
Fiona's just herself, doesn't care
what anyone else thinks.

When my older brother Reuben
volunteered to "chaperon" me,
I was totally onto his game,
but curious to see white girls gawking
at a "fine young Black man,"
as he calls himself, barely thirteen.

At least he's not a total walking
stereotype: digs hockey over hoops.

Exiting the Wild Weed, Jesse Edward Jamison Comments on the Girl Scouts

Well, don't this beat all, little angels
peddling munchies to go with the bag
of primo weed I just scored, to keep
me and Wendy weekend high.

Still, I'm not sure how I feel about kids
getting corrupted, though I bet they know
in which drawer their folks hide the stash:
little dope fiends, like I was at their age.
Or worse, moms and dads turning
their kids on, a generation
of slacker-stoners in the making.

Me and Wendy toke up only on weekends,
though tempting to kick back Thursday nights,
our favorite sitcoms even funnier with a joint.

I remember when I'd bop in from a party
on a Friday night, or from a Saturday date,
Mom and Dad lolling on the sofa,
their eyes going in circles, everything I said
hilarious, and a savaged bag of potato chips
or an empty box of Oreos, or the crumbs
of Mom's Brownies on the coffee table,
along with the dregs of a couple of Cokes,
butts and roaches slimy looking as snails.

I'd climb the stairs, half-wishing they'd share,
half-grateful they were semi-responsible.

Nancy Tolliver Buys Girl Scout Cookies Outside the Wild Weed

My Harold loves these cookies,
and he has so few pleasures, my poor love.
I left him with the hospice nurse—
who whispered it might be better if I bought
some marijuana for him, for pain management—
and drove here fast, and after I bought him
something edible that the owner guaranteed,

"Your guy will feel absolutely no pain for hours,"
I buy Harold three boxes of every flavor,
but fear he'll just stare, with the longing
of Keats in his last, sad days.

How we loved to quote his poems
on our Scottish walking tour in his footsteps,
but ventured farther north, and didn't sleep rough;
clean sheets and a luxurious bath after each day's hike,
Harold massaging my soles with his all-knowing fingers.

Keats had his companion Severn place books around
his last bed in Rome, so if he couldn't read them,
could at least feel their beauty and wisdom seep
from their pages into his brain, heart, and soul.

Maybe that's what Harold wants, now that everything
tastes of ashes, though I pray this marijuana
and these cookies will magic a cure for my darling.

Thomas Bickerstaff Buys Girl Scout Cookies Outside the Wild Weed

It's about time,
but they're thinking too small,
like, well, like little girls,
and not a man with big ideas.

If it were me, and it will be,
they'd be selling all kinds
of munchies, not just cookies,
but brownies, marinara sauce,
and all of it laced with pot,
plus T-shirts, posters
of pop divas in Scout uniforms,
a button or two undone,
to show bodacious ta-ta's,
to appeal to stoners,
who get so crazy on a few tokes
they need instant gratification.

I almost feel like tossing away
the lid I just bought,
to concentrate instead,
on creating a company name,
logo, a marketing strategy,
and to find suppliers, designers,
seamstresses, to make *tchotchkes*
to my specifications.

Free enterprise! Capitalism!
Selling everything to everybody!
What makes this country great!

Teddy Levine, on Line to Buy Girl Scout Cookies

Jesus-freakin'-Christ,
this woman's taking all day,
can't make up her mind,
so she's demanding free
samples of every variety.

The girls behind the table
roll their eyes, but afraid
to tell her to screw off,
so the scout leader informs her,
with a smile tight as a dolphin's
rear end in a rip tide,

"I'm so sorry; we can't
break open boxes."
Madam Entitled stalks off
as if a butcher had tried
to pass off gristle for T-bone.

Finally, it's my turn!
But I forget what I want,
the kids snickering
like I'm already stoned,
which, I confess, I am, a little.

I point, while the ounce
in my pocket gets hot
as a fired .45 on old TV westerns,
when cowboys rode off
into the sunset, free as mustangs,
and schoolmarms waved goodbye
and tried not to weep,
not like Becky and me.

Teri Gambier Buys Girl Scout Cookies

Girl Scout cookies will go great
after my secret stoner spaghetti sauce:
the cookies an ironic comment
on the sauce, the perfect meal
for a third date: nudgerooni.

Gary's a sexy guy who doesn't
even realize it, with his shy smile,
and startled, but very pleased look,
when I laid a long, wet one
on him on our second date.

These kids are so adorable,
though it makes me a little sad;
I wonder how many have found
their parents' stashes, not
that I was much older
when I took my first toke,
and coughed my brains out.
Mom scared the be-Jesus out of me:
threatening to turn me in,

"So you'll rot in prison forever,"
and I was dumb enough to believe her.

I met Gary cute, as they say,
in the Whole Foods: me, eyeing
the last chocolate chip cannoli,
Gary—the perfect gentleman,
seeing me stare like I hadn't eaten
in centuries—gave up his place
to me; the rest, history.

Or it will be, if everything
goes as planned tonight.

Gerald Lockhart Walks Past the Wild Weed Dispensary

Kids bopping out of the Wild Weed
think they invented dope.
So stupid-easy to score: just pick
a mellow trip or a mind fuck,
like buying a Sauvignon or a Cab.

And Girl Scouts shilling cookies outside?
You know it tempts kids to smoke,
and Jeez, I sound like my Republican
old man, may he rest in peace.

But hell, back in the day, you earned
your high: shitting bricks walking past
beat cops, pretending there were only books
in our book bags, like we were smuggling
forged identity cards for the Underground,
if that isn't a sacrilegious comparison
for what that generation had to go through,

all to make the country safe for Trump
to turn the U.S. into a hate-filled state.
But forget Tangerine Mussolini;
it's these kids who piss me off,
not having to work for their weed,
like we did, when sex, drugs,
and rock 'n' roll meant something.

Jeremy Lind, Buying Girl Scout Cookies

Marijuana? Smells like every skunk
in the state let loose a stink bomb:
what led to Ella leaving, accusing
I never wanted to try anything new.

"God, you're such an old man!
Where's your sense of adventure?"

Adventure? Rafting down
the Devil's Punchbowl is adventure;
hiking Long's Peak is adventure.
With pot, all you do is cough and giggle:
little to laugh about, when love's
fickle as a kitten's claws.

But I do love Girl Scout cookies,
always look for the kids setting up
tables outside supermarkets
or at mall entrances.

So I stand in line now, scowl
whenever someone bounces out
of the Wild Weed with a smirk
and a stuffed brown paper bag.

I love all the flavors, but Thin Mints?
Man, that little snap when you bite,
the mint and chocolate mingling,
better than the hippie incense
Ella used to reek up our house with,
her and her friends all laughing,
getting off on how square I was.

Square? That means "dependable."
Exactly the kind of person
this world needs more of.

Amelia Cross Buys Marijuana at the Wild Weed

Give me a fudge brownie
or a fistful of Mrs. Fields,
to go with the bumble-bee buzz
of some righteous weed.

I hate the Girl Scouts,
after what I went through
with those smiling bitches,
who had me in tears, with,

"You look pretty, for a hippo, Amy."
Or, "You've got enough steel
in your mouth for a prison's
barbed wire fence, Amy."
Or, "Is that your hair or an army
of worms on top of your head, Amy?"

When I'd come home sobbing,
Mother never forgave me for not
being the perfect pretty princess,
like all the other girls.
I was the fatso desperate for love;
when that was never going to happen.

So I stomp past the Scouts now,
a look of murder to make them step back;
not a sales pitch peep out of the witches.
Anyway, I can bake better cookies:
my secret ingredient?
That's why it's secret.

Trey Winslowe, with Bad Intentions, Outside the Wild Weed

What are all these Girl Scouts
doing outside the Wild Weed,
shilling cookies like pushers?
How am I supposed to pull my piece
and stick a ski mask over my face,
with little girls in the line of fire?

Don't the Scouts have any sense?
What kind of message is that:
letting kids hang outside a pot shop
like it's the corner candy store?
If I had a daughter, I'd make damn sure
she wasn't subjected to all this stuff
that can twist her faster than hot tar
turns sneakers into getaway smears
for any moron-cop to follow,
like the undercover one keeping
well back as I retreat, but man,
he is so freakin' obvious and I ain't
done nothin', just had a look or two.

Maybe Friday, right before closing,
if I can wait that long: students
stocking up for party night and hot dates.
And aside from the stuffed till,
there'll be a ton of weed
to scoop up and sell on the street,
where lots of heads still prefer to buy,
thinking themselves outlaws sticking it
to the Man, when I'm the real desperado.

Detective Malcolm Sanders, Sensing More Trouble Outside the Wild Weed

The bulge under his windbreaker,
a dead giveaway; plus that wolf-hungry,
pissed-off look that scumwad thieves
get when their plans turn to shit.

I thought it best to watch and wait;
drawing my piece might've triggered
a blood bath, and besides the guy just
shrugged, slapped his frustrated sides
and stalked away.

I ambled after, until he got into his beater
and drove off, maybe sensing me,
but he didn't peel out, didn't cut off
oncoming traffic, obviously a pro;
I'd made a note of his plate number,
wondered if he'd stolen an inconspicuous
drive he'd ditch when out of sight.

Besides, Kelly needs me: her mom's split,
the usual police story: the hours, the danger,
the creepy gun in the house, the cop slang
that reduces everyone to perps and vics:
a secret society you'd not want to join
even if they begged you.

Nick Breeze, Owner of the Blue Rose Tattoo
Parlor: Denver

"The Girl Scouts Cookie Locator lists sales sites that have been approved by Girl Scouts of Colorado…. This weekend's listings include bars, a tattoo parlor…and a marijuana dispensary."

—The Denver Post

Girl Scout Cookies? Perfect for pot shops,
but my guys are hardcore bikers into
nastier treats, though I gotta admit,
these kids' smiles—like the world's
all gum drops and rainbows—
might make my guys spring for cookies;
and Sonny Bartlett, a wiry little fucker
with a mean streak long as the border
we gotta protect from the Mexicans,
had me ink in a glass of milk and a plate
of his favorites, Peanut Butter Patties:
in honor of his kid that Jo-Jo won't let him see,
backing up the court order with a sawed-off.

Sonny hoped the tat would soften her up.
Not Jo-Jo, who I've been balling.
If Sonny found out, me and her'd be hammered,
and I don't mean drunk, 'less I get to him first,
with my forty-ounce Louisville Slugger
and my sweet, Trevor Story swing.

Cindy Bartlett, Girl Scout and Daughter of a Biker

Other kids have normal parents with 9 to 5 jobs.
Mom a tattoo "artist," like it's anything close
to Picasso or Rembrandt: how she hooked up
with the owner; plus she packs a sawed-off,
for if Daddy tries to kidnap me, or just say hi.

When Daddy visits, he roars up on his hog
to scare the whole neighborhood. I don't know
how Mom faces him down, but she does,
and Dad rides off, pissed.

Now, while we sell cookies, Mom stands guard,
about as conspicuous as Kelly's dad, an off-duty cop.
Mom's packing, to protect me, and Kelly's dad carries
too; if Daddy shows up, oh, it's too scary!

Not that Mom's a saint, seeing that sleaze-bag
Nick Breeze, her boss: so much ink on them both,
they're walking graffiti walls; at least he doesn't
shoot me weird looks, like Mom's other boyfriends,
who I wouldn't stay in the same room with,
for all the cash, guns, and drugs
Daddy used to hide in our basement.

Like I said, I just want a normal childhood.

Joan, Jo-Jo, Bartlett, Observes Her Girl Scout
Daughter Cindy

This street's too open, too easy for Sonny
and his biker buddies to grab Cindy.
Why I'm packing, eyes search-lighting,
ears straining for a hog-roar, while I chat
nonchalant as Bugs Bunny with other parents:
Kelly's cop dad's got his service piece;
I hope he's better with it than other pigs,
who panic-spray bullets like sunflower seeds.

Sonny thinks he's badass Sonny Barger:
the biker who scared the crap out of the world
when the Angels killed that kid at Altamont in '69,
caught in that documentary about the Stones.
Not that I was even born then, but it's biker lore:
Easy Rider with a happy ending for low riders.

I smile, legal herb's cut into Sonny's business,
though he's got tentacles in meth and demon-opioids:
one more reason why I kicked him out.

Enough dreaming. I've made sure Cindy's not near
a gutter, where Sonny can swoop in like stretching
for a carousel ring. I can reach her in two strides,
fire off two fast rounds, though don't want
to turn the sidewalk into a battle zone,
but I'll leave a bloody trail of bodies a mile long,
if I have to, to protect Cindy.

Sonny Bartlett on His Motorcycle, Passes the Wild Weed

Impossible to grab Cindy, other Scouts
all around her, my wife standing guard nearby,
obvious she's packing, and shit, one dad's
an off-duty cop, his service piece holstered.

If I didn't care about collateral damage,
I'd roar onto the sidewalk, snatch Cindy,
and scatter kids and parents like pigeons
flapping into the sky at a pit bull's charge.

People claim us low riders ain't nothing
but white supremacist-neo-Nazis.
Hell, I'm just an American patriot.
And yeah, we stray into retail enterprises
that ain't legal, but just scratching an itch:
meth, coke, smack: what customers want,
now that the state undercuts my weed prices.

That don't mean I don't love my daughter,
and wouldn't've stayed with my wife,
if she'd been the least bit reasonable
about a man's needs, versus what a woman
claims she won't put up with.

Should've had all my bros in battle formation.
Jo-Jo and some lame-ass cop would've had
as much chance as lambs against a wolf pack,
and Cindy'd love wind whipping her hair
while she held on tight to her old dad.

When Jo-Jo spotted me, she smirked
oh so superior and aimed her index-finger-gun;
I lit out faster than the Pony Express.
Damn, that woman got my goat, yet again,
but just you wait, bitch; just you freakin' wait.

Cindy Bartlett Watches Her Father Ride Off

Daddy tried to grab me just now,
and make me live with him
and his biker buddies, but when
he saw Mom, and that Mr. Sanders
with a holstered gun, he revved
his Harley like he was chased by Indians.

Like I'd really have fun hanging
with Daddy and some guys
whose idea of a good time is fighting.
And who knows what those weirdos
might do if they got drunk or stoned,
which is like every single day!

Still, I'd like to spend a quiet afternoon
with Daddy, ride into the mountains,
or hike, in Mt. Falcon Park, maybe see
a mountain lion or bear in the distance.

Or he could just take me to the zoo,
which Mom never has time for,
between tattooing customers and her boss
she's all lovey-dovey with, these days.

I don't know who has more tattoos,
Daddy or Mom's new boyfriend.
At least Daddy wears his biker jacket
over the ink. Mom's guy's arms are thick
as blue, red, and black sausage casings.

Gross!

Rebecca Charters Drives Home

What a day! Little girls
yowling like alley cats
to be let into the dispensary
to try some grass,
as if one toke or bite
wouldn't have knocked them
on their little asses for a week.

And you hear stories about kids
getting into their parents' edibles
and, thinking it's candy, a few
overdosed, and in one case, died,
the poor parents and the guilt
they'll take to their graves!

Then there was that one guy
who looked like he'd rob the dispensary,
had the street been less clogged
with kids and parents. Luckily,
he wasn't totally depraved
and saw Kelly's cop dad's
very unconcealed concealed weapon.

Then to top it all off,
Cindy's biker father buzzed by,
looking to kidnap her, but left,
maybe a twinge of conscience
for little girls who might get caught
in the crossfire between him,
his ex-wife, and Mr. Sanders.

Lord, I need Cecily's hugs,
some pizza, a case of Chardonnay,
and a joint: my reward
for nothing horrible happening.

But if they ever ask me to let my girls
sell cookies outside a pot shop again—
forget the "dispensary" euphemism—
it's, 'No way, nuh-uh, no sirree!'

About the Author

Robert Cooperman's latest collection is *The Ghosts and Bones of Troy* (Aldrich Press). His latest chapbook, *All Our Fare-Thee-Wells,* is forthcoming from Finishing Line Press. Other recent collections are *Lost on the Blood-Dark Sea* (FutureCycle Press) and *My Shtetl* (Logan House Press). Cooperman lives in Denver with his wife Beth.

Made in the USA
Columbia, SC
13 June 2021